ELEGANT
ENTERTAINING
SEASONAL RECIPES
FROM THE AMERICAN AMBASSADOR'S RESIDENCE IN PARIS

ELEGANT
ENTERTAINING
SEASONAL RECIPES
FROM THE AMERICAN AMBASSADOR'S RESIDENCE IN PARIS

DOROTHY WALKER STAPLETON

Executive Chef PHILIPPE EXCOFFIER

Photography FRANCIS HAMMOND

Flammarion

EXECUTIVE EDITOR
Suzanne Tise-Isoré

TRANSLATED FROM THE FRENCH BY
Carmella Abramowitz-Moreau
and Deke Dusinberre

GRAPHIC DESIGN
Bernard Lagacé

FOOD STYLING
Isabelle Clément-Dreyfus

STYLING
Eva Paquin

EDITORIAL COORDINATION
Nathalie Chapuis

COPYEDITING
Helen Woodhall

PROOFREADING
Marc Feustel

PRODUCTION
Angélique Florentin

IMAGE RETOUCHING
Christophe Glaudel

COLOR SEPARATION
IGS, Angoulême, France

Printed in Singapore by Tien Wah Press

Distributed in North America
by Rizzoli International Publications, Inc.

Simultaneously published in French as
À la table de l'ambassadeur, les recettes
de la résidence de l'ambassadeur américain à Paris
© Flammarion, Paris, 2009
English-language edition
© Flammarion, Paris, 2009

87, quai Panhard et Levassor
75647 Paris Cedex 13
editions.flammarion.com

09 10 11   3 2 1
ISBN-13: 978-2-08-030116-1

Dépôt légal: 09/2009

FRONT COVER Asparagus charlotte and avruga.
BACK COVER Iced cognac soufflé and wild strawberries.
PAGES 2–3 Courtyard façade of the American
Ambassador's Paris residence.

Contents

Introduction

NUMBER 41 RUE DU FAUBOURG SAINT-HONORÉ IS LOCATED IN THE HEART OF PARIS, JUST a few yards from France's presidential palace. This glamorous address is the site of a hidden treasure. Parisians as well as tourists often pass by the monumental street entrance without realizing that behind it stands one of the finest examples of a heritage jointly shared by two nations: the hôtel de Pontalba, now the official residence of the United States ambassador to France. An invitation is required in order to enter this nineteenth-century *hôtel particulier*, or private mansion, with a vast garden in the rear that stretches as far as avenue Gabriel. Every year, that privilege is extended to several thousand leading individuals—statesmen, politicians, diplomats, artists, and so on—who are allowed a leisurely look at these magnificent premises. Here Franco-American friendship is celebrated every day, usually around a dining table, sampling the best that French and American gastronomy have to offer when they join forces. An official residence enables an ambassador to receive his or her guests personally, whether the occasion entails hundreds of guests or just a handful. In Paris, where more than sixty U.S. ambassadors have served over the past two centuries, strengthening ties by hosting dinner parties has been a tradition ever since the first ambassador, Benjamin Franklin, was here from 1779 to 1785. In those days an extremely rich aristocrat, Jacques-Donatien Le Ray, who was an unshakeable supporter of the American revolutionaries yet close to Louis XVI, placed his lavish residence in Passy, just outside Paris, at Franklin's disposal. There Franklin did a good deal of entertaining in order to rally the French to his cause, and he ultimately obtained the backing of the French king.

French cuisine was already a sophisticated art in the late eighteenth century, and would soon be popularized by gourmets such as Antheleme Brillat-Savarin and Alexandre Grimod de La Reynière, then perfected by famous chefs such as Antonin Carême. Franklin's successor in Paris, Thomas Jefferson (ambassador from 1785 to 1789), loved French food and especially French wine. Even before coming to France, Jefferson discovered French cuisine as a young heir to a large Virginia plantation, notably at the Governor's Palace in Williamsburg, where he was often a guest in his student days. He could therefore fully indulge this passion when posted to Paris. He did so out of duty as much as pleasure—at that time, French cuisine was the number-two diplomatic language, outranked only by the French tongue itself.

RIGHT Designed by the architect Félix Langlais, the grand staircase in the entrance hall is of seventeenth century classicist inspiration. The sober white limestone contrasts strongly with the many colors of the various types of marble flooring, creating a typically nineteenth-century setting.

FOLLOWING DOUBLE PAGE The decorations and wooden paneling in this salon come from the *hôtel particulier* of Louis XV's famous banker, Jacques Samuel Bernard; the salon, in fact, now bears his name. The room was assembled by a workshop of artists whose art embodied the tastes of the Age of Enlightenment.

Jefferson arrived in France accompanied by one of his slaves, James Hemmings, who was instructed to learn the local cookery and then provide his master's guests with it. The new ambassador moved into an elegant residence on the Champs-Élysées known as the hôtel de Langeac; the landlord was Louis XVI's younger brother, the comte d'Artois, who would later become King Charles X. The residence boasted twenty-four rooms and, most important, a fine garden. Indeed, Jefferson had an idea that would take hold and flourish down the present day: he would not only treat his guests to French cuisine, but would also introduce them—most diplomatically—to American specialties unknown on this side of the Atlantic. That is why he imported and planted in his Paris garden not only Newtown Pippin apples, which in his opinion were superior to all French apples, but also corn, sweet potatoes, watermelons, cranberries, and so on. Similarly, he impressed his guests with imported products such as Virginia hams, which he felt were better than anything found in Paris.

After four years as ambassador, which included the start of the French Revolution, Jefferson parted from his many French friends (including Lafayette, Condorcet, and Du Pont de Nemours) and returned to the United States to resume his famous political career. His luggage was packed with a variety of French delicacies that he wanted to share with friends at home, namely mustard, vinegar, cheese, olive oil and no less than 680 bottles of fine wine. He introduced other leading Americans to these pleasures, thereby communicating his love of France to the very top of the young government, as witnessed by a letter he wrote to the comte de Lur Salaces, owner of the already glamorous château d'Yquem, shortly after his return home. "The white wine of Sauternes of your cru, that you were kind enough to send to me in Paris in early 1788 has been so well accepted by Americans who know good wines that I am sure that now that I am back in the United States my countrymen here will admire them. Our President, General Washington, would like to try a sample. He would like for you to send him thirty dozen, sir, and for myself I would like to have ten dozen."

Over two centuries ago, then, the tastes of these two friendly nations were already mingling, serving as a vector for economic and cultural ties. The gourmet Jefferson provides striking proof that local gastronomy has long been the best way to engage with a stranger, to establish a bond of friendship. Since ancient days there have been countless treaties and agreements that were negotiated not in a formal setting, but rather during a banquet, around a table laden with delicacies. Such was the case at the Congress of Vienna, which took place from November 1814 to June 1815 and laid the foundations for the Europe that existed up to the First World War. France's chief negotiator, Talleyrand, went to Vienna with his chef, Antonin Carême, and hosted banquet after banquet in the Kaunitz Palace, which he had rented. Talleyrand managed to have French brie crowned "king of cheeses" despite stiff competition from English stilton and Dutch limburger. Meanwhile, Metternich, the Austrian representative, made a hit with his pastry chef, Franz Sacher, who invented the famous chocolate *sachertorte* for the occasion. Thus the nineteenth-century map of Europe

RIGHT The grand staircase, with its wrought-iron banister, leads to the salons. The architect's intention was to maintain a relatively muted tone until the visitor entered the richly decorated and furnished rooms of the house.
FOLLOWING DOUBLE PAGE To the left of the lobby, the octagonal salon was decorated by Baron Edmond de Rothschild around 1880. It is decorated with exceptional Regency woodwork from the Parisian hôtel particulier of Madame Peyrenc de Moras, today the Rodin Museum. The octagonal salon leads to the cloakroom, which holds three paintings by William Bouguereau (1895–1905), of which *L'Amour* (Love) is shown here.

was more or less drawn on the dinner table. As Carême wrote, "the art of cuisine goes with diplomacy, and every Prime Minister is dependent on it." A similar idea was expressed a century later in another aphorism, attributed to the great chef Auguste Escoffier, inventor of Peach Melba, Pear Belle-Hélène, and Crêpes Suzette: "The art of cooking is perhaps one of the most effective forms of diplomacy."

Thomas Jefferson's example was followed by his successors in Paris. His friend James Monroe, U.S. ambassador from 1794 to 1796, was already a fervent connoisseur of French cuisine when he arrived in Paris. Some ten years earlier, Monroe and Jefferson shared not only a house in Annapolis, but also a caterer, a certain Monsieur Partout. Monroe therefore pursued the tradition of culinary exchange instituted by his predecessor. In 1817, having been elected the fifth president of the United States, Monroe purchased for the White House over fifty pieces of French Empire-style furniture made by Pierre-Antoine Bellangé, cabinet-maker to Napoleon.

FORTY-FIVE AMBASSADORS FOLLOWED MONROE BEFORE ARTHUR K. WATSON AND HIS WIFE moved into the entirely restored hôtel de Pontalba in January 1972. (In the meantime, U.S. ambassadors to France had lived in various residences, the most recent being 2 avenue d'Iéna.) Twenty-four years earlier, in 1948, the American government had decided to buy the Pontalba property from Baron Maurice de Rothschild to house the offices of the U.S. Information Service. By taking ownership of this magnificent residence, then in dilapidated condition, the United States took stewardship of its eventful history.

During the reign of Louis XIV, this neighborhood was a *faubourg*, or outlying village, on the edge of Paris. It was called Faubourg Saint-Honoré, and rich financiers and influential statesmen began buying up land and building fine mansions there. One of them was Joseph-Antoine d'Aguesseau, a counselor to the Paris *parlement* who, upon dying childless, bequeathed his fine property and home to his brother, Royal Chancellor Henri-François d'Aguesseau. In the early nineteenth century, this property at 41 rue du Faubourg Saint-Honoré still belonged to a descendent of the Aguesseau brothers, Marquise Marguerite de Boigelin. In 1836, aged twenty-seven, the marquise sold it to a colorful character, Micaela Amonester y Roxas, Baroness de Pontalba. The baroness was a rich heiress of a Spanish notary, Andrès Almonester y Roxa, who had made a fortune in real estate in New Orleans, where she was born and grew up, and where her father died in 1798 when she was just three years old. Micaela was fifteen when her mother's cousin, Baron Joseph Delfau de Pontalba—also born in New Orleans but resident in France for fifteen years—arranged her marriage to his son Célestin. Célestin and his mother sailed across the Atlantic, and the wedding was held in New Orleans in October 1811. The newlyweds then returned to

ABOVE In the Franklin bedroom, a bust of Benjamin Franklin by sculptor Jean-Antoine Houdon (1741–1828) is a reminder of his importance in the history of Franco-American relations. Benjamin Franklin was the first American representative to be sent to France, where he stayed from 1776 to 1785. He led the negotiations by which France gave official recognition and support to the newly born nation.

RIGHT A detail of an engraving drawn after a painting by Hobens of Franklin's reception at the court of France in 1778.

FOLLOWING PAGE, LEFT
Top left: A famous art lover and patron of the arts, Baron de Rothschild showcased his fabulous collection of paintings and rare objects in his *hôtel particulier*. Top right: Main façade of the *hôtel particulier* built by the neo-classical architect Louis Visconti for Baroness de Pontalba. It underwent changes in 1876. Bottom: The "Lacquer Salon," which takes its name from the precious lacquer-covered walls, showcased Baron de Rothschild's furniture and *objets d'art*. It is now known as the Pontalba Salon.

FOLLOWING PAGE, RIGHT
Portrait of the Baroness de Pontalba.

France and moved into the baron's château in the Oise region north of Paris. Despite the birth of three children, the couple's marriage was not a happy one, spoiled by financial disputes between the baron and Micaela's mother. The conflict continued to worsen, and ended in a tragic manner: on October 19, 1834, Baron de Pontalba shot his daughter-in-law with a pistol. Two bullets struck Micaela in the chest and another two hit her left hand as she tried to protect herself. She nevertheless managed to flee, at which point the baron shot himself. The bloody incident was all the talk of Paris, where it was suggested that the father-in-law was trying to defend his son's honor in the face of his daughter-in-law's infidelity. Stendhal, who was staying in Italy at the time but who regularly read French newspapers, alluded to the incident in a letter to a friend dated November 8th: "Those idiotic political papers only stoop to anecdote when there's blood; that's how I read of the affair; I know husband and wife. Who was the protagonist, the indirect cause of all this mess?"

Micaela recovered and it took a court case against her husband before she finally regained personal control over her fortune. She managed the money brilliantly, investing in housing construction in New Orleans, including the Pontalba townhouses, built on Jackson Square in the late 1840s, today some of the oldest apartment houses in the United States. Two years after the shooting she also bought, in Paris, the property at 41 rue du Faubourg Saint-Honoré. Not wanting to keep the various existing buildings, she hired one of the best architects of the day, Louis Visconti, to build a new mansion. Masterminded by Visconti but heavily influenced by the baroness's own refined tastes, the building campaign lasted several years. Micaela notably concentrated on the interior—and sometimes exterior—decoration of the home, using items that she purchased herself in old stately homes. Thus magnificent lacquer wall panels that had graced the residence of the duc de Maine on rue de Lille in Paris in the early eighteenth century found their way into her interior. She similarly purchased several pediments, here and there, to decorate the exterior façades. By the early 1840s, the splendid hôtel de Pontalba was finally finished and flaunted a highly elegant eighteenth-century-style interior for the receptions given by the baroness.

Micaela died in 1874. Two years later, Baron Edmond de Rothschild, aged thirty-two, purchased the mansion from her heirs. The youngest son of the famous banker James de Rothschild, Edmond was a great art lover who left management of the family business to his brothers so that he could devote most of his life to his art collection and patronage. He commissioned Félix Langlais, the family's official architect, to transform the Pontalba residence. The only things the architect left untouched were the gatehouse and portal, both dating from the eighteenth century. Langlais's main contribution was the construction of two wings, which gave the building its current H-shaped floor plan. Rothschild commissioned a major revamping of the interior—new features included a majestic main staircase, an octagonal salon with woodwork acquired from a mansion near Les Invalides (now the Musée Rodin, to which the baron later returned the woodwork), new decoration in the ballroom (with carved

PRECEDING DOUBLE PAGE Between 1878 and 1888, the Rothschilds had the ballroom extended towards the garden, and built a gallery to connect it to the cloakroom. Their architect, Félix Langlais, installed the sculpted woodwork representing scenes from the *Fables* of Jean de La Fontaine, taken from the *hôtel particulier* of Samuel Bernard, Louis XV's banker.

RIGHT The Louis XVI salon, decorated with fine interlaced design in what is known as Etruscan style, testifies to the classical taste of the time of Baroness de Pontalba. On the red marble fireplace stands a magnificent clock with typically baroque decorative elements.

FOLLOWING DOUBLE PAGE Important dinners, receptions, and cocktails are held in the official dining room. Its eighteenth-century wooden paneling was acquired by Baron de Rothschild and comes from a number of Parisian *hôtel particulier*.

Résidence de l'Ambassadeur des États-Unis en France

Dinner & Dancing to Celebrate
Franco - American Friendship

Tomate confite en surprise
Crabe et avocat
...
Noisette d'agneau provençale
Tian de légumes pommes Darphin
...
Assiette de fromages de France
...
Pompon orange chocolat

Condrieu" La Solarie" Barge 2007
Corton "Clos du Roi" Grand Cru Senard 2002
Stapleton & Springer Saint Laurent Craig's Reserve 2006
Magnum Champagne Ruinart Blanc de Blanc

Samedi 11 Octobre 2008

woodwork inspired by La Fontaine's *Fables*), and, in one of the drawing rooms, magnificent woodwork that had belonged to Louis XV's banker, Jacques Samuel Bernard. The crucial transformation, however, was the installation of the baron's extraordinary, teeming collection of furniture, old-master paintings, prints, and manuscripts, which turned the residence into a miniature Louvre.

Edmond de Rothschild bequeathed part of his collection to various institutions, including the Louvre. His son Maurice, who inherited the mansion, had time just before World War II to remove a few other treasures. The Rothschilds sought refuge in Switzerland prior to the arrival of the Germans. The hôtel de Pontalba was immediately requisitioned by Hermann Goering, who used it as the Luftwaffe headquarters, meanwhile confiscating the remaining artworks. Some of these works were recovered after the war by the Seventh U.S. Army, and returned to their owners. The Rothschilds, however, no longer lived in the hôtel de Pontalba. After the Liberation of France, Maurice de Rothschild briefly rented it to the British Royal Air Force Club, then sold it to the United States government in 1948.

⁘

IT WAS THUS AN ELEGANT AND GLAMOROUS, IF SLIGHTLY MUTILATED, BUILDING THAT housed the U.S. Information Service. In addition to most of the furnishing and artworks, the parquet floors had vanished, along with the historic woodwork and wrought-iron banisters and balustrades. In 1966, however, the U.S. government decided to move its ambassadorial residence from avenue d'Iéna to the mansion on rue du Faubourg Saint-Honoré; the press and information services were transferred to the hôtel Talleyrand on place de la Concorde. A vast renovation and decoration program, scheduled to last five years, then got underway, supervised by architects Pietro Belluschi and Ernest Barlow. Five years of work finally returned the hôtel de Pontalba to its former luster in 1972. The recovery of certain original features took longer—some of the lacquer panels that had vanished from the Pontalba salon were rediscovered after a lengthy search and re-installed in 2001. The restoration was generously supported by The Friends of 41, a group of American art patrons who donated many works of art and decoration in order to replace those that vanished after the departure of the Rothschild family.

Even as they restored precious features to their original state whenever possible, the decorators incorporated, as harmoniously as possible, allusions to several grand symbols of Franco-American friendship. A library was founded—the Jefferson Library—and filled with furnishing and books that evoked the former ambassador and third president of the United States who so loved France; bedrooms were named after Franklin, Lafayette, and Charles Lindbergh, being specially decorated with portraits and mementos of the men who built bridges between the two nations.

RIGHT Chef Philippe Excoffier spends as much time working in the kitchens as he does in his office, where he creates his outstanding dishes and menus. **FOLLOWING DOUBLE PAGE** The kitchens of the ambassador's residence hold an impressive collection of gleaming pots and pans in which delicious dishes are prepared.

The bed in which Lindbergh slept immediately after his historic transatlantic flight on May 21, 1927, is now in the room that bears his name.

Among the very rare house guests at the hôtel de Pontalba, the most prestigious is obviously the president of the United States, for whom a bedroom is reserved. In contrast, the number of guests invited to a luncheon, dinner or reception at the ambassador's home runs into the tens of thousands every year. The occasions are too numerous to list, ranging from a concert of American music to a conference of non-governmental organizations, via a symposium with French artists and intellectuals, or a tasting of American wines, not to mention major American holiday celebrations such as Independence Day and Thanksgiving, to which the Marines stationed at the embassy are also invited, and the ambassador's private dinners, for visiting friends or colleagues.

In order to delight the palates of all these guests, the ambassador can depend on the renowned talent of the Residence's Executive French chef, Philippe Excoffier. After earning his stripes at two glamorous three-star restaurants—the Restaurant Pic in Valence and Lucas Carton (Alain Senderens) in Paris—Excoffier became the head chef at the residence of the American chargé d'affaires in 1998, then at the ambassador's Residence two years later. His credo reflects the golden rule of French gastronomy: respect the rhythm of the seasons, using fresh market produce to its best advantage. Yet even once that principle has been adopted, coping with the type of reception and number of guests—which differ every day, sometimes several times a day—still constitutes a brain-racking task, often compounded by last-minute changes.

Hence action is always preceded by reflection, imagination, and anticipation. Excoffier spends as much time in his "command center" as he does before the ovens. Next to the vast kitchens gleaming with a splendid collection of copper pots and pans, his office has walls dotted with handsome, constantly changing sketches of ideas for dishes and their colorful presentation on the plates of delighted guests. "The kitchen staff arrives every morning at 7:30," says the chef. "We begin by inspecting the produce purchased the day before, which has been delivered during the night. If the quality of anything is unsatisfactory, we send it back, hoping that the high-quality produce will arrive in time. And we often face other uncertainties—loss of electrical power or cooking gas, or a significant change in the number of guests. The team is accustomed to these minor problems, like a well-oiled machine that knows it can't afford to choke whatever happens. Soon everyone is at work, slicing, mixing, whipping, simmering, and adjusting, so that the end result is picture perfect. The goal is always the same: serve the finest possible meal right on time—the ambassador's luncheons start at 1:00 p.m., sharp.

"In the afternoon, everything begins all over again for dinner. First we make the sauces and side dishes, we prepare the meat, and we see to the desserts. During this time, the maître d' will oversee the laying of the tables. The seating plan is a problem

LEFT Every day, Philippe Excoffier and his team prepare all the breakfasts, lunches, and dinners for the embassy.

that always has to be resolved with tact, since the success of an event largely depends on it. Next, the kitchen team is allowed to take a break. But not me, because I have to remain focused on what follows. And this is the moment that I can draw up suggested menus for the ambassador's wife, with whom I meet regularly. Together we plan the menus for the next week's lunches and dinners, drawing inspiration from seasonal produce. We also take into account the harmony of flavors and textures, and we devise attractive presentations. I make notes of her recommendations, for example a light first course followed by a main dish with a colorful garnish, then a gourmet dessert. After our meeting, I go back to my office and order things from my suppliers. Then I gather the team for a set of final instructions and we get back to work."

Ever since Ambassador Craig Stapleton imported a barbecue from the United States and launched the tradition, every September a garden barbecue is held at the Residence. This typically American, friendly and relaxed way of enjoying food is highly appreciated. Once the chef and his staff discovered what a real American barbecue was, they immediately adopted it as their own, obviously contributing their own "French touch." As Excoffier recalls, "For our first barbecue we were expecting several hundred guests. We had no idea what preparing this kind of meal for so many people involved. Given that difficulty, I reassured my team, '*Can't do* is not French!' And I started looking up the best American barbecue recipes, which we then prepared in a French manner. We served potato salad, coleslaw, and grilled chicken, not forgetting of course hamburgers, hot dogs and our now-famous lemon bars and brownies. The ambassador was delighted and congratulated me by telling me I'd become a 'great Franco-American chef.'"

Excoffier fully deserves this compliment, being a sophisticated diplomat and expert chef who knows how to discreetly perpetuate the long-standing friendship between two great countries. But readers can judge for themselves, because here the chef is inviting them to discover and prepare some of the seasonal dishes that have orchestrated receptions at the Residence during annual parties and events for honored guests.

RIGHT The ambassador welcomes guests—dignitaries, artists, intellectuals, and friends from the USA—in a manner befitting the elegant surroundings. The salons with their tasteful floral bouquets and dinners comprising inventive menus all bear out the careful attention that hallmarks the Residence.

SUMMER

Summer in France is a riot of fresh fruit and vegetables. Their bright colors flood outdoor markets in cities as well as villages, flaunting not only the bounty of their vitamins but also their wonderful, refreshing, often naturally sweet taste. At last tomatoes are the real thing again, reminding us that they are a fruit, not a vegetable! Peaches and apricots melt in the mouth, almost intoxicatingly succulent. Capsicum peppers, eggplant, new potatoes, fresh garlic, and young onions accompany meat and fish, sometimes enlivened with spices. All these sunny flavors stimulate Excoffier's imagination, yielding light, refreshing dishes that bring color to a summer table.

In the Residence, distinguished guests staying in the Lafayette Room, decorated with several period portraits of the great man, rise and prepare for breakfast, after which they will stroll through the garden before returning to the cool of the mansion's lofty historic rooms.

RIGHT AND FOLLOWING DOUBLE PAGE The garden of the residence stretches out to avenue Gabriel. Originally designed as a garden *à la française* with geometrical flower beds, it was gradually modified by its successive owners to become a landscaped English garden. In the nineteenth century, Baroness de Pontalba had a small shed built at the foot of a large tree.

FOURTH OF JULY★ GARDEN PARTY

The Independence Day celebrations on the Fourth of July are naturally the main social event of the year. On that day over two thousand guests are invited to the Residence, draped for the occasion in enormous star-spangled banners. The chef spends months preparing this garden party, for he must encourage guests to appreciate the wide variety of American cooking with its countless local specialties, from the traditional Western barbecue to Louisiana's Creole dishes via other regional favorites—New England crab cakes, Pacific salmon, bread pudding with Kentucky bourbon sauce, New Orleans shrimp fritters with guacamole.

A few other major events also require lengthy preparation on the part of the chef and his team. The Paris Air Show, for example, provides an occasion, organized every two years by the Department of Commerce, for over one thousands guests to sample American food and wine. On a recent menu was Wagyu beef from Nebraska, whose quality matches its direct rival, the famous Kobe beef from Japan.

RIGHT Throughout the year, the ambassador welcomes guests of note and holds many receptions, including one to commemorate the Independence of the United States. The Fourth of July is the major event.

Traditional American cooking holds the limelight at the garden party held on the Fourth of July. Chef Philippe Excoffier has his own take on popular dishes like hamburgers and barbecued food, offering both French and American guests the best of what American gastronomy has to offer, presented *à la française*.
FOLLOWING DOUBLE PAGE On Independence Day, the Marines who guard the embassy are invited to celebrate the national holiday. For this major annual event, the American and French flags are unfurled on each side of the second floor window, and they float from the garden façade to pay tribute to France, the very first ally of the United States of America.

During the celebrations for the Fourth of July, musicians set the tone for the festivities when the star-spangled banners are unfurled by the Marines of the embassy. Traditional music and swing-filled jazz, fifes and resounding trumpets commemorate the history of the United States of America.

FOLLOWING DOUBLE PAGE In the private dining room, the ambassador hosts dinners for visiting friends and colleagues. The solid mahogany table is stamped by the cabinet maker Canabas. Of exceptionally large proportions, it holds three revolving trays. Between the two windows, nestling in a niche, a copy of the ancien Roman sculpture of Diane of Gabies (the original work is in the Louvre Museum) adds tranquility and elegance to this room.

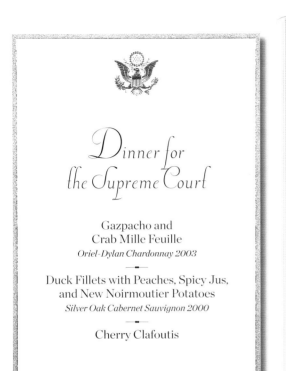

STARTER FOR 6
PREP 30 minutes
COOK 10 minutes
RESTING TIME 2 hours

FOR THE GAZPACHO
6 large tomatoes
1 red bell pepper
1 green bell pepper
1 stalk celery
1 small cucumber, peeled and seeded
2 garlic cloves
3 ¹/₂ tablespoons (50 ml) olive oil
3 ¹/₂ tablespoons (50 ml) balsamic vinegar
3 ¹/₂ tablespoons (50 ml) sherry vinegar
1 teaspoon (5 ml) Tabasco sauce
2 tablespoons tomato paste concentrate
Salt and pepper to taste

FOR THE MILLE FEUILLES
2 sheets brick or 4 sheets phyllo pastry
3 ¹/₂ tablespoons (50 ml) olive oil

FOR THE TARTAR
1 carrot
About 20 stems chives
1 shallot
Zest and juice of 1 lime
2 oz. or 3 ¹/₂ tablespoons (50 g) mayonnaise
10 oz. (300 g) crab flesh
¹/₄ bunch dill

1 ¹/₄ oz. (35 g) avruga
(Spanish herring roe) for garnish

Gazpacho and Crab Mille Feuille

First prepare the gazpacho. Wash all the vegetables and cut them into pieces. Place them in a mixing bowl with the olive oil, vinegars, Tabasco, tomato paste concentrate, and salt and pepper. Marinate for 2 hours in the refrigerator. Stir all the ingredients together and filter through a sieve. Chill.

Preheat the oven to 300°F (150°C).

Brush the sheets of pastry with the olive oil. Cut out 18 disks, 2 ¹/₂ in. (5 cm) in diameter. Place them between two baking trays so that they remain flat and bake for 10 minutes. Remove from the oven and set aside.

Finely dice the carrot. Snip the chives and the shallot. In a bowl, combine the carrot cubes, chives, shallot, lime zest and juice, mayonnaise, and crab flesh.

Place 1 oz. (30 g) portion of tartar on a pastry disk and cover with a second disk. Place another equal portion of tartar on this, and top with a third disk of pastry. Pour the chilled gazpacho into soup plates and place a crab mille feuille in the center. Garnish with a scant teaspoon of avruga and a few dill sprigs and serve immediately.

Duck Fillets with Peaches, Spicy Jus, and New Noirmoutier Potatoes

MAIN COURSE FOR 6
PREP 30 minutes
COOK 50 minutes

3 yellow peaches
2 tablespoons (40 g) honey
1/4 cup (60 g) unsalted butter
3 shallots
1 head garlic
1 sprig thyme
3 bay leaves
10 oz. (600 g) small new potatoes from Noirmoutiers (Bonnotte variety or other small, thin-skinned potatoes)
3 tablespoons (45 ml) olive oil
6 fillets of young duck

FOR THE SAUCE
2 tablespoons plus 1 teaspoon butter
3 shallots, finely sliced
Scant 1/2 cup (100 ml) sherry vinegar
2 1/2 tablespoons (50 g) honey
1 teaspoon five-spice powder
3 star anise
3 oz. (100 g) wild cranberries
2 cups (1/2 liter) duck or veal stock

To prepare the sauce, melt the butter in a skillet and gently fry the sliced shallots over low heat. When they are softened, pour the vinegar over and bring to the boil. Add the honey, spices, wild cranberries, and stock. Reduce the liquid by half. Set aside.

Blanch the peaches for a few moments in boiling water, then dip them into a large bowl of cold water. Peel them and cut them into halves, removing the pits. Cut into quarters. Heat the honey in a pan and place the peach quarters in it for a few minutes to color them on each side. Set aside.

Preheat the oven to 350°F (180°C). Cut the shallots into halves and cut the garlic head in half crossways. Melt the butter in a cast-iron pot with a heatproof lid. Add the shallots, garlic, thyme, bay leaves, and potatoes, unpeeled. Cook over a high heat until golden, then cover with the lid and place in the oven for 20 minutes.

Put the olive oil into a skillet and color the duck fillets over low heat for 4 to 5 minutes, removing the excess fat as it exudes. Place the duck fillets on an ovenproof tray and roast in the oven, still at 350°F (180°C), for 7 minutes.

Switch off the oven, leave the door ajar, and allow to rest for 4 minutes before slicing the duck breasts.

Reheat the sauce over a low heat. Arrange the duck fillets, potatoes, peach slices, and sauce on plates and serve immediately.

Cherry Clafoutis

DESSERT FOR 6

PREP 20 minutes

BAKE 20 minutes

³/4 lb. (350 g) cherries
¹/4 cup (20 g) ground hazelnuts
³/4 cup plus 1 ¹/2 tablespoons (85 g)
all-purpose flour
1 ¹/2 teaspoons (5 g) potato starch
¹/4 cup (50 g) sugar
1 heaped tablespoon (15 g)
vanilla sugar
3 eggs
1 cup (250 ml) milk
1 cup (250 ml) whipping cream
¹/3 cup (80 g) butter,
melted until brown
Scant ¹/2 cup (100 ml) kirsch

FOR THE BAKING PAN
1 tablespoon (15 g) butter, softened
A little sugar for sprinkling

Preheat the oven to 400°F (200°C).

Pit the cherries and set aside. Combine the ground hazelnuts, flour, potato starch, sugar, and vanilla sugar. Beat in the eggs. Slightly warm the milk and cream together and incorporate them into the mixture. Add the browned butter and the kirsch and beat very well.

Butter a mold 10 in. (25 cm) in diameter with a pastry brush and sprinkle it with sugar. Pour the clafoutis batter into the pan. It should not be more than three-quarters full to allow room for the batter to rise. Scatter the cherries over the batter. Place the pan on a baking tray and bake for about 20 minutes until golden and risen.

FOLLOWING DOUBLE PAGE The ambassador's official dining room is decorated with a magnificent eighteenth-century Flemish tapestry illustrating a scene from the life of Moses, the Adoration of the Golden Calf. The tapestry is attributed to Gaspard Van der Borght.

Duo of Tomato and Goat Milk Cheese, Salad of Baby Shiso, and Basil Pesto

STARTER FOR 6
PREP 30 minutes
COOK 15 minutes
CHILL 2 hours

6 Roma tomatoes
3/4 lb. (350 g) fresh goat milk cheese
3 1/2 tablespoons (50 ml) olive oil
1/2 teaspoon fresh chopped garlic
1/2 teaspoon ground thyme
Salt and pepper to taste

FOR THE BASIL PESTO
2 sheets (4 g) gelatin (see page 156)
2/3 cup (150 ml) cup olive oil
1 bunch basil, washed, leaves picked
1 garlic clove, peeled
1 oz. (30 g) pine nuts, lightly toasted

1 cup green shiso leaves
1 cup red shiso leaves

Pre-heat the oven to 200°F (90°C). Place the tomatoes in boiling water for 30 seconds and peel them. Cut them into quarters, removing the core and seeds. Oil a baking sheet and arrange the tomato segments. Brush them with olive oil and sprinkle with the thyme, chopped garlic, and salt and pepper. Roast the tomatoes for 15 minutes.

For the Basil Pesto, soak the gelatin sheets in a bowl of cold water for 5 minutes. Remove and squeeze out the water thoroughly.

Heat the olive oil well in a saucepan. Process the basil leaves, garlic clove, and pine nuts in the bowl of a food processor, and the heated oil and mix. Incorporate the gelatin and process again to incorporate. Pour the mixture into a rectangular dish and chill to set.

Break up the goat milk cheese using a fork.

For the most attractive presentation, use a stainless steel pastry ring 2 1/2 in. (6 cm) in diameter. Cut out circles from the pesto-gelatin layer using the pastry ring. Arrange two segments of tomato in the circle, followed by a layer of goat milk cheese, a layer of set pesto, and another layer of goat milk cheese. Finish with a layer of tomato segments. Repeat to make the other 5 duos. Chill for at least 2 hours before serving. Arrange the tomato-cheese duos on 6 plates and garnish with the shiso leaves.

Baked Line-Caught Sea Bass with Marjoram Vegetable Jus

MAIN COURSE FOR 6

PREP 20 minutes

COOK 10 minutes

2 x 2 lb. (1 kg) sea bass, scaled and gutted (ask your fishmonger)
1 head garlic
1 cup (250 ml) olive oil
5 sticks dried fennel
Few sprigs thyme and 1 bay leaf
Salt and pepper to taste

FOR THE VEGETABLE JUS
2 carrots
1/2 onion
2 shallots
2 stalks celery
2 tomatoes
2 tablespoons (30 ml) olive oil
3 star anise
1 cup (250 ml) fish stock
1/2 bunch marjoram

First make the vegetable jus: peel the carrots and slice them into rounds. Peel and finely slice the onion and shallots. Finely slice the celery stalks. Cut the tomatoes into quarters and de-seed them. Gently fry all the vegetables in the olive oil for 5 to 6 minutes, then add the star anise, the fish stock, and the marjoram. Cook for 30 minutes. Remove the star anise and the marjoram, blend and strain the liquid through a coarse sieve.

Preheat the oven to 350°F (180°C). Cut the garlic head in two crossways. In a large pan, color the fish in olive oil for five minutes on each side, together with the garlic, dried fennel, thyme, and bay leaf. Season with salt and pepper. Place the fish in an ovenproof dish and bake for 10 minutes.

Serve the sea bass with the vegetable jus.

Puff Pastry Fantasy of Melon and Watermelon with Apricot Sorbet

SERVES 6

PREP 20 minutes

BAKE 14 minutes

1 lb. (500 g) puff pastry
¹/3 cup (50 g) confectioners' sugar
1 large cantaloupe melon
¹/4 watermelon (4–5 lb. or 2–2.5 kg)
Lemon verbena, to garnish
1 pint tub (500 g) apricot sorbet

Preheat the oven to 350°F (180°C).

Roll out the puff pastry. Cut out 6 disks of 4 in. (10 cm) diameter.
Place them between two baking trays and bake for 14 minutes.
Dust with confectioners' sugar as soon as you remove them from the oven.

Cut the cantaloupe melon in half and remove the seeds.
Using a scoop with a diameter of about 1 in. (2 cm), prepare balls
of cantaloupe and watermelon.

Arrange the fruit on the puff pastry, alternating cantaloupe
and watermelon. Garnish with lemon verbena.

Serve with the apricot sorbet.

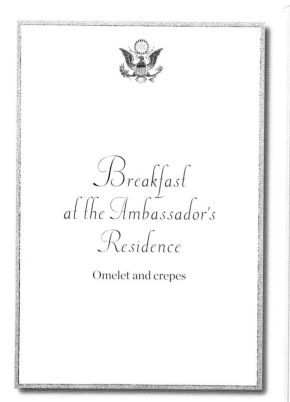

Breakfast at the Ambassador's Residence

Omelet and crepes

SERVES 6
PREP 15 minutes
COOK 30 minutes

18 eggs (3 eggs per person)
3 ¹/2 tablespoons (50 ml) sunflower oil
Salt and pepper to taste

SERVES 6
PREP 10 minutes
COOK 20 minutes

5 eggs
1 ¹/2 tablespoons (20 g)
granulated sugar
2 teaspoons (10 ml)
pure vanilla extract
2 cups (¹/2 liter) milk
2 ¹/4 cups (200 g
all-purpose flour, sifted
Scant ¹/2 cup (100 g) butter,
melted
Oil, for frying

Omelet and crepes

OMELET

Break 3 eggs into a small mixing bowl and beat well.
Season with salt and pepper.

Heat a little oil in a pan and pour in the beaten eggs.
Cook for 2 minutes. To ensure even cooking, use a spatula
to push the cooked edges inward as the omelet starts to cook,
allowing still-liquid egg to run onto the bottom of the pan.
Leave on the heat for a further 2 minutes, then fold over
and turn onto a plate. Repeat for the other 5 omelets.

Serve immediately.

CREPES

Beat the eggs together with the sugar and the vanilla extract
in a mixing bowl. Add the milk, beating continuously, then the sifted
flour, and lastly the melted butter. Allow to rest for 30 minutes.

Heat the oil in a small pan and cook the crepes until light golden.
Flip over and cook on the other side.

Serve with sugar, preserves, or any other accompaniment
of your choice.

RIGHT AND FOLLOWING DOUBLE PAGE The presidential bedroom overlooks
the garden. The large ornamental cornice decorated with trophies
of musical instruments was built by the Rothschilds. The furnishings
and fabrics in peach and yellow tones are in eighteenth-century style.

FALL

Autumnal colors—rust, old leather, brandy, ebony, and mahogany—
awaken the taste buds to mineral flavors. This is the season of
undergrowth where numerous kinds of mushrooms gather and truffles
hide in fragrant leaves and damp moss after the rain. The fall is also rich
in smoky tastes, in peanuts and chestnuts. All these colors, scents, and
tastes come together in an autumn bonfire. On rue du Faubourg Saint-
Honoré, there is no better season for settling down in the Jefferson
Library, where the warm shades of woodwork, the old book bindings,
and the silk curtains echo the reddening leaves in the garden. But it is
time to head for the table on this fourth Thursday in November.
Tonight Philippe Excoffier has revisited the traditional Thanksgiving
meal, adding his usual light touch. A tender capon has replaced
the usual turkey, and the apple pie is served upside-down,
in the so-called *Tatin* style.

RIGHT AND FOLLOWING DOUBLE PAGE Several exotic trees, including
North American sequoias and Japanese maples, grow in the garden
of the ambassador's residence. Two gardeners work every day
on the upkeep of this oasis of greenery nestling in the heart of Paris.

STARTER FOR 6
PREP 25 minutes
COOK 20 minutes

Scant ¹/2 cup (100 ml) olive oil
1 pack of brick or phyllo sheets
1 head curly endive
1 Granny Smith apple
1 ¹/2 oz. (40 g) truffle
12 cherry tomatoes
2 lb. (900 g) porcini
3 garlic cloves
1 cup curly-leaf parsley
2 tablespoons (30 g) butter
3 shallots, finely sliced
1 bunch chervil
Salt and pepper, to taste

SPECIAL EQUIPMENT
12 small round baking molds

Porcini Croustade

Preheat the oven to 350°F (180°C).

Brush a sheet of brick with oil and place another sheet over it. Brush with oil. (If using phyllo pastry, which is thinner than brick pastry, use 4 sheets layered on top of each other.) Using a pastry cutter, cut out 6 disks of 4 ¹/2–5 in. (12 cm) diameter.

Arrange the pastry disks in 6 molds of the same diameter and cover the pastry with a mold of the same size to prevent it from rising during baking. Bake for 8 minutes.

Wash the lettuce and dry it. Cut the apple into slices and then into thin sticks. Finely slice the truffle. Cut the cherry tomatoes into quarters and set aside.

Brush the porcini, carefully removing all traces of sand. Cut them into halves. Peel and chop the garlic. Chop the parsley.

Sauté the porcini in a pan with olive oil for 6 minutes, stirring from time to time. Add the butter and garlic and cook for a further 2 minutes. Add the shallots and parsley. Season with salt and pepper and remove from the heat.

Arrange the porcini on the pastry disks. Delicately garnish with the apple sticks, truffle shavings, tips of curly endive leaves, chervil leaves, and cherry tomatoes.

Grilled Tuna, Broccoli Mousseline, and Soy Sauce

Cut the broccoli into small florets and cook in a pot of well-salted boiling water for 8 minutes. Drain and purée them with the cream to make the mousseline. Set aside, keeping warm.

Cut the tomatoes into quarters, remove the core and seeds, and cut into fine strips.

Shell the peas and blanch in a pot of salted water for 4 minutes. Drain. Combine the soy sauce with the first quantity of olive oil and the lime juice. Season with pepper.

Cut each tuna slice into 3 identical rectangles. Season with salt and pepper. Brush them with olive oil and grill them on a ridged cast-iron grill pan for 1 minute on each side.

Arrange the tuna, scoops of broccoli mousseline, peas, and tomato strips in the plates. Drizzle with soy sauce.

Serve immediately.

MAIN COURSE FOR 6

PREP 20 minutes
COOK 15 minutes

5 heads broccoli
3 1/2 tablespoons (50 ml) heavy cream or crème fraîche
12 cherry tomatoes
1 lb. (500 g) garden peas
3 1/2 tablespoons (50 ml) soy sauce
Scant 1/2 cup (100 ml) olive oil, for the sauce
Juice of 2 limes
6 x 5 oz. (150 g) thick slices of tuna
1/3 cup (75 ml) olive oil, for the tuna steaks
Salt and pepper to taste

Menton Lemon Soufflé

Preheat the oven to 350°F (180°C).

Butter 6 small soufflé dishes and dust them with flour.

Beat the egg yolks with the sugar until the mixture turns pale. Add the flour and beat again.

In a saucepan, heat the milk.

Pour half the hot milk over the egg yolks, beating continuously, then add the other half.

Pour all the liquid back into the saucepan, bring to a simmer, and simmer for 2 minutes over low heat. Switch off the heat and add the lemon juice and lime zest.
Whip the egg whites stiffly with the sugar. Delicately fold them into the crème pâtissière and fill the soufflé dishes.
Smooth over with a spatula and bake for 10 minutes.

Serve immediately.

DESSERT FOR 6
PREP 15 minutes
BAKE 20 minutes

4 eggs, separated
3 tablespoons plus 1 teaspoon (40 g) sugar for the egg yolks
2/3 cup (65 g) flour, plus extra for dusting
2 cups (500 ml) milk
Juice of three Menton lemons
(or fairly sweet, Meyer-type lemon)
Zest of 2 limes
1 tablespoon plus 2 teaspoons (20 g) sugar for the egg whites

SPECIAL EQUIPMENT
6 soufflé molds

PAGE 78 The sculpted figures on the dining room table center-piece are part of a collection acquired by President Eisenhower for a luncheon given in honor of President Charles de Gaulle in 1959.
PAGE 79 Detail of a carved panel in the private dining room: the strewn flowers and delicate foliage scrolls are typical of the fine woodwork of the seventeenth century.

STARTER FOR 6

PREP 25 minutes

COOK 30 minutes

1 lb. (450 g) cannelloni, preferably
Barilla
6 leeks
1/4 cup (50 g) unsalted butter
1 cup (250 ml) whipping cream
18 raw langoustines
Olive oil, for sautéing
1 oz. or 2 1/2 tablespoons (30 g)
grated Parmesan
1 handful borage flowers for garnish
Salt and pepper to taste

FOR THE SAUCE VIERGE
12 cherry tomatoes
3 oz. (100 g) black olives
About 15 stems chives
1 small carrot
Scant 1/2 cup 100 ml olive oil,
preferably Kalamata
3 tablespoons (45 ml) balsamic vinegar
1 tablespoon (15 ml) satay sauce

Langoustine Cannelloni with Leeks and Satay-Flavored Sauce Vierge

Prepare the cannelloni in salted boiling water according to instructions on the pack. Drain and dip immediately into cold water. Remove quickly and place them on a clean cloth. Split them lengthways.

Remove the outer skin and the greens from the leeks and discard. Wash the whites thoroughly, and slice finely. Sauté the slices in the butter for 3 minutes. Pour in most of the cream, reserving a little. Season with salt and pepper and leave to simmer for 10 minutes over low heat.

Shell the langoustines and remove the intestine. Sauté them in a skillet with a little olive oil. Season with salt and pepper.

Preheat the broiler. Arrange the cannelloni on a chopping board. Fill them with the leek slices and place a langoustine on the top. Roll the cannelloni into a tube and brush with the remaining cream. Sprinkle with Parmesan cheese. Gratinate the cannelloni for 5 minutes.

Cut the cherry tomatoes into quarters, remove the core and seeds, and slice them finely. Pit the olives and slice them finely. Snip the chives, peel the carrots, and prepare carrot sticks. Combine the olive oil, balsamic vinegar, and satay sauce. Season with salt and pepper and add the cut vegetables.

Arrange the cannelloni on plates, spoon over the satay-flavored sauce vierge, and garnish with borage flowers.

Serve immediately.

Stuffed Medallion of Lamb, Chanterelles, and Truffles

MAIN COURSE FOR 6
PREP 35 minutes
COOK 1 hour 20 minutes

2 saddles of lamb, deboned
and nerves removed, cut into fillets
7 oz. (200 g) caul
(obtain from butcher's
to envelop the medallion)
or kitchen string to tie the medallions
10 oz. (300 g) chanterelles
3/4 cup (200 ml) olive oil
1 3/4 tablespoons (25 g) butter
1 cup (250 ml) lamb jus
2/3 cup (150 ml) truffle jus
6 tomatoes
2 garlic cloves, peeled
3 sprigs thyme and 1 bay leaf
1 truffle weighing 1 1/2 oz. (40 g)
2 large Bintje or Yukon Gold potatoes
Salt and pepper to taste

FOR THE STUFFING
1/2 bunch curly-leaf parsley
1 clove garlic
4 oz. or 1 cup (120 g) breadcrumbs
(packaged)

First make the stuffing: process the parsley with the garlic and add the breadcrumbs. Pulse further until you have a fine consistency.

Season the saddles of lamb with salt and pepper. Butterfly the thicker fillets (the *contre-filets*) so that they are the same width as the other fillets. If using caul, spread it on the work counter and place the lamb fillet on it (otherwise, you will need to tie the medallions more tightly with kitchen string to cook them). Cover the fillet with the breacrumb and parsley mix. Place another on top, roll it up (in the caul, if using), and tie with kitchen string, at close intervals.

Wash the chanterelles. Fry them in a little olive oil for about 3 minutes. Season with salt and pepper. Drain, reserving the liquid.
Put the skillet back on the heat, add the butter, and sauté the chanterelles again for 3 minutes.
Heat the lamb jus. Add the liquid from the chanterelles and the truffle jus. Leave to boil briefly. Keep warm.

Preheat the oven to 200°F (100°C). Dip the tomatoes in boiling water for 1 minute to peel them. Arrange them in an ovenproof dish and slow roast them in the remaining olive oil with the garlic, thyme, and bay leaf for 40 minutes.

Finely slice the truffle. Peel the potatoes and cut them into wedges. Fry them in a deep fryer.
Increase the oven temperature to 350°F (180°C).

Pan fry the saddles of lamb for 2 minutes on each side in some oil. Place them in an ovenproof dish and cook for 8 minutes. Remove from the oven and tent with aluminum foil. Leave for 4 minutes. Remove string and cut into slices.

On each plate, place 2 slices of stuffed saddle of lamb, some chanterelles, a slow-roasted tomato, and some fried potato wedges. Spoon lamb jus over the plates and garnish with truffle shavings.

Serve immediately.

Poached Pear, Caramel Mousse, and Almond Tuiles

DESSERT FOR 6
PREP 30 minutes
COOK 30 minutes
CHILL 2 hours

6 Bartlett pears
Juice of 1 lemon
2 vanilla beans
1/2 cup (110 g) sugar
6 cups (1.5 liters) water
A few mint leaves

FOR THE CARAMEL MOUSSE
Generous 1/2 cup (120 g) sugar
1 cup (250 ml) milk, heated
4 sheets gelatin (see page 156)
3 egg yolks
1 cup (250 ml) whipping cream,
well chilled

FOR THE ALMOND TUILES
1 cup (200 g) sugar
3/4 cup or 2 1/2 oz. (75 g)
blanched chopped almonds
Juice and zest of 1/2 orange
1/2 cup (125 g) butter, melted

SPECIAL EQUIPMENT
6 small molds or pastry rings

Combine all the ingredients for the almond tuiles and chill for 2 hours.

To make the caramel mousse: Place all but 1 1/2 tablespoons (20 g) of the sugar in a small saucepan with 2 tablespoons water and heat. When a dark brown caramel begins to form, gradually pour in the hot milk, stirring continuously. Continue cooking until the caramel has dissolved in the milk.

Soak the gelatin in cold water and drain thoroughly.
Whip the egg yolks with the remaining sugar. Slowly pour the caramel over the egg yolks, beating all the time. Pour the mixture back into the saucepan and simmer over a low heat, stirring constantly, until it thickens and coats the back of a wooden spoon. Stir in the gelatin and pour into a bowl. Allow to cool. Beat the whipping cream and fold it delicately into the cool caramel mixture. Fill 6 molds or pastry rings 2 1/2 in. (6 cm) in diameter and 1 1/4 in. (3 cm) high with the caramel mousse. Chill for 2 hours.
Preheat the oven to 350°F (180°C).

Line a baking tray with parchment paper and make 6 x 1 3/4–2 in. (4–5 cm) diameter disks with the almond tuile batter.
Bake the tuiles until they turn a golden color. Remove from the oven and leave to cool, ensuring that each tuile is flat.
Peel the pears and squeeze a little lemon juice over them so that they retain their color. Split the vanilla beans lengthways in two, scrape out the seeds, and put them in a saucepan. Add 6 cups (1.5 liters) water and the sugar and bring to the boil. Place the pears in the hot syrup and poach gently for 20 minutes. Remove them from the water and allow them to cool.
Turn the caramel mousses out of their molds.
Place a caramel mousse on a plate.
Place an almond tuile above it and top with a pear.

Garnish with mint leaves. Repeat to prepare the other 5 plates.

FOLLOWING DOUBLE PAGE The Jefferson library was established in 1972 for Arthur K. Watson, the first ambassador of the United States of America to take up residence here. It is decorated with Louis XV woodwork and is dedicated to Thomas Jefferson (1743–1826), who was the second American representative to France. The leather armchair on wheels is a copy of one designed by Jefferson himself. The books, all leather-bound, are from the collection of William Short, personal secretary to Jefferson when he was in Paris; they include many works by Voltaire and Rousseau.

Thanksgiving Dinner

Creamed Pumpkin Soup
Vernay Condrieu Vernon 2005

Stuffed Fillet of Capon, Chestnuts,
and Pressed Potatoes
Stapleton & Springer Rouči 2004

Apple Upside-Down Cake My Way
Champagne Krug 1995

STARTER FOR 6

PREP 30 minutes
COOK 15 minutes

4 shallots
3 cloves garlic
4 lb. (2 kg) pumpkin
2 tablespoons (30 ml) olive oil
4 cups (1 liter) chicken stock
1 cup (250 ml) heavy cream
or crème fraîche
1/3 cup (70 g) butter
Salt and pepper to taste

Creamed Pumpkin Soup

Peel the shallots and garlic cloves and slice them finely.
Peel the pumpkin and cut into chunks.

Heat the olive oil in a large pot. Add the shallots and fry gently
for 3 minutes. Add the pumpkin and garlic and fry gently
for a further 5 minutes, stirring from time to time.
Pour in the chicken stock and season with salt and pepper.

Cook the soup for 15 minutes, then add the cream and butter.
Blend in a food processor and strain through a fine-meshed sieve.

Stuffed Fillet of Capon, Chestnuts, and Pressed Potatoes

MAIN COURSE FOR 6
PREP 40 minutes
COOK 2 hours, 35 minutes

2 lb. (1 kg) Charlotte or other fairly firm,
waxy potato
1/2 cup (125 g) clarified butter
6 capon fillets
7 oz. (200 g) caul or enveloping membrane
3 large porcini
Sunflower oil
3 tablespoons (40 g) butter
18 cooked, vacuum-packed chestnuts
Salt and pepper to taste

FOR THE STUFFING
2 oz. or 1/3 cup (60 g) sultanas
1/2 stalk celery
3 dried apricots
1 Granny Smith apple
1 onion
1/2 bunch parsley
1/4 cup (60 g) butter
3/4 cup (150 g) brown sugar
1 cup (250 ml) chicken stock

FOR THE CRANBERRY SAUCE
1 lb. (450 g) fresh or frozen cranberries
2 oranges, peeled, white pith removed,
and cubed
Zest of 1 orange
1 cup (250 ml) orange juice
2 cups (500 ml) water
2 sticks cinnamon
3 1/2 oz. or 2/3 cup (100 g) sultanas
3/4 cup (150 g) brown sugar
1 apple, peeled and diced
2 oz. or 1/3 cup (60 g) orange marmalade

SPECIAL EQUIPMENT
6 Dariole molds
(small, steep-sided cylindrical molds)

Begin with the cranberry sauce. Place all the ingredients in a pot and simmer gently for 1 1/2 hours, with the lid on.

Then make the stuffing. Plump the sultanas in a little water.

Finely dice the celery stalk and dried apricots. Peel the apple and dice it.

Peel the onion and slice it finely. Wash and chop the parsley.

Sauté the onion in a skillet with butter for 5 minutes. Add all the other stuffing ingredients except the parsley. Pour in the chicken stock and cook, covered, for 15 minutes. Incorporate the parsley and turn off the heat.

Preheat the oven to 350°F (180°C). Peel the potatoes and cut them out using a cutter to obtain cylinders of a diameter identical to that of your mold. Slice them finely using a mandolin or sharp knife. Place them in a bowl and pour over most of the clarified butter. Arrange the potato slices in layers, filling the molds. Then pour over the remaining butter. Bake for 35 minutes.

Open the capon fillets lengthways, ensuring that you do not cut right through. Spoon in generous portions of the stuffing, close up, wrap in caul, and tie with string.

Clean the porcini and cut them in halves. Sauté them in a skillet for 6 minutes with a little oil, salt, and pepper. Add 1 1/2 tablespoons (20 g) butter and cook for 1 minute more. Remove from the heat and keep warm.

Lower the oven temperature to 300°F (140°C). In a skillet, sauté the capon fillets in the remaining butter for 3 minutes on each side. Place them in an ovenproof dish and cook for 16 minutes. Leave the oven door ajar and allow to rest for 5 minutes.

Heat the chestnuts in a little water in a saucepan.

Cut each stuffed capon fillet into 4 slices.

On each plate, arrange 2 slices of capon, a dariole of pressed potatoes, half a porcini, some chestnuts, and cranberry sauce.

Serve immediately.

Apple Upside-Down Cake My Way

To make the pastry, combine the flour, sugar, coconut,
and salt by hand. Add a little cold water and the cubed butter.
Work into a ball. Leave to rest for 1 hour at room temperature.
Preheat the oven to 325°F (160°C).
Roll the pastry out to a thickness of about ¼ inch (4 mm)
and place in a 10-in. (24 cm) diameter cake pan. Bake for 20 minutes.
Raise the oven temperature to 350°F (180°C). Peel the apples
and cut them into quarters. Remove the cores. Heat the sugar and butter
in a skillet until the mixture turns a light caramel color. Place the apple
quarters in the skillet and cook them for 3 minutes on each side.
Arrange them in a second 10-in. (24 cm) diameter baking tin
and pour the caramel over. Bake for 30 minutes.
Remove the apples from the oven and place the baked pastry over them.
Return to the hot oven for 8 minutes.
Turn the upside-down cake out of the cake pan and serve immediately.

SERVES 6

PREP 25 minutes
BAKE 65 minutes

10 to 12 Golden Delicious apples
½ cup (100 g) sugar
Scant ½ cup (100 g) butter at
room temperature, cubed

FOR THE PASTRY
1 ½ cups (125 g) flour
⅓ cup (60 g) sugar
3 tablespoons dried shredded
coconut (unsweetened)
⅓ cup (90 g) butter
Pinch of salt

RIGHT AND FOLLOWING DOUBLE PAGE The dining room has three massive mahogany
tables known as "dumb waiters" because of their three revolving trays.
It also holds two marble and gilded wood Louis XV consoles.

WINTER

In the garden of the Residence, only the leaves of the evergreen sequoias resist the wintry chill. But the kitchen is good and warm, because Excoffier is preparing a great French specialty—exquisite scallops. Scallop fishing is highly regulated in Brittany and Normandy, and the seasons runs from October to April. The kitchen staff is hard at work with a range of winter fruit and vegetables that provides a wide variety of flavors. France is a country where local produce is appreciated and protected. The AOC label (Appellation d'Origine Contrôlée), once limited to great wines, has now been extended to other produce as a guarantee of authenticity. The Puy region's famous green lentils, the first vegetable to earn this honor, are a favorite winter dish. It is also the season for endives, cabbage, onion soup, caramelized turnips, and other delights. When it comes to fruit, French-grown citrus fruit, apples, and pears are joined by pineapple and bananas from overseas. They often light up desserts, rivaling the finest winter treat—chocolate.

RIGHT AND FOLLOWING DOUBLE PAGE In winter, the bare flowerbeds in the gardens of the ambassador's residence resemble abstract works of art. The exterior appears to be asleep, but within the salons, activity and receptions continue.

*Luncheon for
the French President*

Lobster, Celery Rémoulade, and Potatoes
with Tonka Bean Sauce
Newton Vineyard Chardonnay Red Label 2004

⚬

Quail in Cabbage Leaf
with Simmered Lentils
Château Montelana, Cabernet Sauvignon 1992

⚬

Honey Caramelized Pineapple,
French Toast, and Vanilla Ice Cream
Château d'Yquem 1976

STARTER FOR 6

PREP 25 minutes

COOK 10 minutes

6 x 1/4 lb. (250 g) lobsters
3 large Bintje or Yukon Gold potatoes
3/4 teaspoon (2 g) ground Tonka bean,
divided
1 celeriac
Juice of 1 lemon
2 oz. or 3 1/2 tablespoons (50 g)
mayonnaise
2 teaspoons (10 g) mustard
1 x 1 1/2 oz. (40 g) truffle
Scant cup (230 ml) olive oil, plus a
drizzle to cook the potatoes
3 1/2 tablespoons (50 ml) balsamic
vinegar
1 shallot, finely sliced
Borage flowers, to garnish
4 sprigs dwarf basil, to garnish
Salt and pepper to taste

Lobster, Celery Rémoulade, and Potatoes with Tonka Bean Sauce

Steam the lobsters for 5 minutes in a steam cooker.
Shell them and cut them into regular, round slices.

Peel the potatoes. Prepare small potato balls using a scoop.
Boil them in a saucepan of boiling water with a little olive oil, salt,
and half of the ground Tonka bean for 5 minutes.

Peel the celeriac and cut it into fine julienne strips. Place the julienne
in a bowl. Squeeze lemon juice over it and combine it with
the mayonnaise and mustard to make a remoulade.
Slice the truffle and use a cutter to make small truffle disks.

Combine the olive oil, vinegar, finely sliced shallot, and the remaining
ground Tonka bean. Season with salt and pepper.

Arrange the celery remoulade in a circle in the center of the plates.
Place the lobster slices on top, overlapping them slightly.
Place the potato balls around the plate and drizzle with the vinaigrette.
Garnish with truffle disks, borage flowers, and a sprig of dwarf basil.

Quail in Cabbage Leaf with Simmered Lentils

MAIN COURSE FOR 6

PREP 40 minutes

COOK 1 hour

1 green cabbage
Fillets of 6 quails
3 carrots
12 pearl onions
4 1/2 tablespoons (50 ml) olive oil
Butter, for braising
1 cup (250 ml) strongly flavored chicken jus
1 bunch sage

FOR THE STUFFING
2 chicken breasts
1 pinch nutmeg
1 egg white
2/3 cup (150 ml) heavy cream or crème fraîche
Salt and pepper

FOR THE LENTILS
10 oz. or 1 1/2 cups (300 g) green lentils, preferably Puy lentils
1 carrot
1 onion
4 1/2 tablespoons (50 ml) grapeseed oil
1 bouquet garni
2 cups (500 ml) chicken stock
Salt and pepper

Place the lentils in a pot of salted water and bring to the boil.
Allow to boil for 3 minutes. Drain and rinse.
Peel the carrot and dice finely. Peel and chop the onion.
Gently fry the onion and carrot cubes in a pot with the grapeseed oil
for 5 minutes over medium heat. Stir from time to time.
Add the lentils, bouquet garni, and chicken stock. Season with salt and pepper.
Leave to simmer for 20 minutes with the lid on.

Take 6 large, very green cabbage leaves. Wash them and blanch them
in a pot of salted boiling water for 3 minutes. Remove from the pot
and refresh them in a large bowl of iced water.
For the stuffing, cut the chicken breast into pieces. Place them in a food
processor with salt, pepper, a pinch of nutmeg, and the egg white.
Process thoroughly, add the cream, and process again. Set aside.
Rapidly sauté the quail fillets on each side. Season them with salt and pepper.

Prepare six pieces of plastic wrap and place a cabbage leaf on each one.
In the center, place a quail fillet and spoon some of the chicken stuffing over.
Place another quail fillet over it. Repeat the procedure for the other
five portions.
Wrap the meat completely in the cabbage leaf to form a ball.
Wrap the balls in plastic wrap.
Peel the carrots and scoop out the flesh with a very small scoop.
Blanch the carrot scoops in boiling salted water for 4 minutes.
Peel the pearl onions and braise them in a pan with a little oil, butter,
and a little water for 20 minutes over very low heat. Stir from time to time.

Heat the chicken jus with a few sage leaves.
Leave to infuse with the lid on for 5 minutes. Filter the liquid.
Steam the stuffed quail fillets for 8 minutes.
Remove the plastic wrap and cut each roll in half.
Spoon a circle of hot lentils into 6 plates. Place 2 half-rolls of quail
in cabbage leaf on the lentils, together with two pearl onions.
Garnish the plates with carrot scoops and sage leaves.
Pour a little sage-flavored chicken jus over the meat, lentils, and vegetables.
Serve immediately.

Honey Caramelized Pineapple, French Toast, and Vanilla Ice Cream

Peel the pineapple, carefully removing the eyes. Cut it into thin slices, under ¼ in. (1 cm) thick. Melt the butter in a pan and lightly color the pineapple slices on both sides. Pour in the honey, turning the slices over several times in the butter-honey mixture for 2 minutes. Pour in the orange juice, bring to the boil, and set aside to cool.

Cut the brioche into 6 slices. In a large mixing bowl, whisk the eggs, egg yolk, and sugar until the mixture becomes pale. Cut the vanilla bean lengthways into two. Scrape the seeds into the bowl. Add the milk, cream, and cinnamon to the mixing bowl and beat again.

Heat the grapeseed oil in a skillet. Soak 3 slices of brioche in the egg mixture, turning them over. Place in the skillet and lightly brown them. Turn over and brown on the other side. Remove the slices from the pan and place them on paper towel to drain. Repeat the procedure with the 3 other slices.

Serve the caramelized pineapple slices with the brioche and a scoop of vanilla ice cream.

DESSERT FOR 6

PREP 20 minutes

COOK 15 minutes

1 pineapple
3 1/2 tablespoons (50 g) butter
4 tablespoons (60 ml) honey
Juice of 1 orange
6 scoops good-quality vanilla ice cream

FOR THE FRENCH TOAST
1 brioche loaf weighing 10 oz. (280 g)
2 eggs
1 egg yolk
3 1/2 tablespoons (40 g) sugar
1 vanilla bean
1 cup (250 ml) milk
3 1/2 tablespoons (50 ml) whipping cream
1/2 teaspoon ground cinnamon
Scant 1/2 cup (100 ml) grapeseed oil

STARTER FOR 6

PREP 25 minutes

COOK 35 minutes

6 Belgian endives
3 1/2 tablespoons (50 g) butter
3 1/2 tablespoons (50 ml) olive oil
18 scallops
1 eggplant

FOR THE CREAMED WATERCRESS
1 leek
1 bunch watercress
3 cloves garlic
3 1/2 tablespoons (50 g) butter
2 shallots, finely sliced
2 cups (500 ml) chicken stock
1 cup (250 ml) crème fraîche
or heavy cream
Salt and pepper to taste

Seared Scallops, Softened Belgian Endives, and Creamed Watercress

To make the creamed watercress, clean the leek thoroughly and slice thinly. Wash the watercress and remove most of the stems. Peel the garlic cloves and slice finely.

Melt the butter in a pot and add the shallots, leek, and garlic. Sauté for 5 minutes, stirring from time to time. Pour in the chicken stock and cook until reduced by half. Add the cream and bring to the boil again. Add the watercress and cook for a further 5 minutes. Season with salt and pepper. Blend the liquid and strain through a fine sieve into a mixing bowl. Place this into a larger bowl with cold water and ice cubes to refresh.

Cut the Belgian endives in half, remove the core, and cut finely. Melt the butter in a frying pan and add the Belgian endives. Cook over a high heat for a few minutes until golden. Remove from heat and keep warm.

In another skillet, heat the olive oil well and sauté the scallops for 2 minutes on each side. Using a mandolin, slice the eggplant lengthways. Cut the slices in two lengthways and fry in hot oil for 5 minutes to make chips.

Pour the creamed watercress into 6 soup plates. Arrange the Belgian endives and 3 scallops on each plate. Garnish with the eggplant chips.

Serve immediately.

PRECEDING DOUBLE PAGE The lights from the windows on the garden façade indicate that within, people are busy late into the night.

Salmon with Zucchini Scales and Champagne Sauce

Prepare the poaching liquid. Peel and slice the carrots.
Peel the garlic and cut the cloves in half.

In a fish kettle, bring the white wine to the boil with $6\frac{1}{3}$ cups (1.5 liter) water, carrots, garlic, celery, bouquet garni, olive oil, and kosher salt. Once it comes to the boil, leave to simmer gently for 10 minutes.

Cut the zucchini in half lengthways and slice finely.
Blanch the slices for 1 minute in salted boiling water.
Drain and dip into a bowl of iced water, and drain again.

Place the salmon in the poaching liquid and bring to a simmer.
Leave to cook over low heat for 13 minutes.

Remove the salmon from the fish kettle. Remove the skin from the body of the fish, leaving the head and tail intact.

Arrange the zucchini slices on the back of the salmon:
start from the tail, overlapping them slightly, and work toward the head, so that they resemble scales.
For the sauce, melt the butter in a saucepan and add the sliced shallots. Sauté gently for 3 minutes. Pour in the champagne and leave to reduce by half. Add the cream and season with salt and pepper. Leave to boil for 4 minutes and then strain the sauce through a fine sieve.

Serve the salmon hot with the champagne sauce.

MAIN COURSE FOR 6
PREP 30 minutes
COOK 35 minutes

1 carrot
2 garlic cloves
4 cups (1 liter) white wine
1 stalk celery
1 bouquet garni
3 $\frac{1}{2}$ tablespoons (50 ml) olive oil, preferably Kalamata
1 oz. (30 g) kosher salt
3 zucchini
1 x 3 lb. (1.4 kg) salmon, gutted

FOR THE SAUCE
3 $\frac{1}{2}$ tablespoons (50 g) butter
3 shallots, finely sliced
4 cups (1 liter) champagne
1 cup (250 ml) heavy cream or crème fraîche
Salt and pepper to taste

FOLLOWING DOUBLE PAGE The Salmon with Zucchini Scales and Champagne Sauce.

DESSERT FOR 6

PREP 40 minutes

COOK 25 minutes

CHILL 2 hours

FOR THE JOCONDE PASTRY BASE
6 egg yolks
1 1/2 cups (290 g) sugar, divided
7 oz. or 2 cups plus 6 tablespoons (200 g)
blanched ground almonds
Generous 3/4 cup (75 g) flour
6 egg whites

FOR THE PRALINE MOUSSE
2 oz. (50 g) milk chocolate
1 3/4 tablespoons (25 g) butter
7 oz. (200 g) hazelnut paste
3 1/2 oz. (100 g) "Feuillantine" (crushed caramel
waffle wafers)

FOR THE CHOCOLATE MOUSSE
1/3 cup (70 g) granulated sugar
9 egg yolks
10 oz. (350 g) bittersweet couverture
chocolate (65%)
2 cups (500 ml) whipping cream

FOR THE GLAZE
2/3 cup (140 ml) water
Scant cup (180 g) sugar
Scant 1/2 cup (110 g) whipping cream
1/2 cup (60 g) unsweetened cocoa powder
3 1/2 sheets (7 g) gelatin (see page 156)
Crystallized flowers, to decorate, optional

SPECIAL EQUIPMENT
1 deep metal pastry ring, 10 in. (25 cm) in diameter

Creamy Caribbean Dessert

Preheat the oven to 350°F (180°C). To make the Joconde pastry base, pulse the egg yolks, half the sugar, the ground almonds, and the flour for 4 minutes in a food processor. Whip the egg whites with the remaining half of the sugar and fold into the mixture. Line two baking trays with parchment paper. (You will need to make two disks 10 in. [25 cm] in diameter later.) Spread the batter over the baking trays and bake for 15 to 20 minutes until light golden.

Now prepare the praline mousse. In a saucepan, melt the milk chocolate with the butter. Remove from the heat and add the hazelnut paste and the crushed wafers. Pour this into the pastry ring and chill.

To prepare the chocolate mousse, place the sugar and 3 tablespoons (45 ml) of water in a saucepan. Heat until the liquid begins to thicken, taking care it does not color. Beat the egg yolks with an electric beater until pale. Pour the sugar syrup over the egg yolks, beating constantly until cold. Melt the couverture chocolate in the microwave oven at medium power, 15 seconds at a time, stirring at intervals, until it is smooth and completely melted. Set aside to cool. Whip the cream with an electric beater and fold it in to the chocolate. Carefully incorporate the egg-yolk mixture.

Carefully unmold the praline mousse from the pastry ring. Cut out two disks of Joconde pastry base the same size as the ring. Place one at the bottom of the ring and pour in a third of the chocolate mousse. Place the disk of praline mousse above this, followed by another third of the chocolate mousse, then the second disk of Joconde pastry. Finish with the remaining chocolate mousse.

Chill for at least 2 hours.

To make the glaze, boil the water, sugar, and cream for 10 minutes in a saucepan. Add the cocoa powder and remove from the heat. Soften the gelatin sheets in cold water for 5 minutes. Remove and wring out the water before incorporating them into the glaze. Leave the glaze to cool.

Remove the metal ring and glaze the cake with a smooth metal spatula. Place on a serving dish.

FOLLOWING DOUBLE PAGE *The Flame of Liberty* was placed in the garden in 2008. The statue, over twelve foot high, was created by French artist Jean Cardot, who also made monumental sculptures of General de Gaulle and Winston Churchill. It was commissioned by a number of important American and French people who work towards strengthening the ties between the two countries. On the base, one can read a quotation by the Marquis de La Fayette: "Humanity has won its battle, liberty now has a country."

PRING

"I love Paris in the springtime" goes the Cole Porter song. It was the season chosen by Charles Lindbergh for the first airplane flight across the Atlantic. The young, spirited aviator—ever-present in the Residence thanks to the memento-filled room that bears his name—here symbolizes spring as much as the flowerbeds of lilac, poppies, and roses. It is the season of love and liberty, of May-pole dances, and of the long-awaited ripening of strawberries—especially wild strawberries, those tiny but fleshy and fragrant berries still commonly found in Europe.

The chef sometimes includes flowers in his colorful compositions, such as cornflowers in spring vegetables served with an herb sauce. Worth mentioning are not only potatoes, sorrel, and radishes, but also tender asparagus, whose short May season must be exploited to the hilt, plus the highly aromatic morille mushroom found in April and May. Everything in spring is light, delicate, fleeting—Excoffier's dishes lend the palate an impression of plenitude and delight in the passing moment.

RIGHT A detail of the garden façade. In 1966, the U.S. government decided on a five-year restoration plan. They had occupied the residence for some twenty years already, and wanted to restore the building to its former glory. Under the supervision of several architects, the splendid woodwork and decorative elements were rediscovered and restored.

Dinner for an Art Award

Prawn, Mango
and Green Apple Salad
Château Montelena Chardonnay 1997

—•—

Sole Wafer with Morel Mushrooms
and Beurre Blanc Sauce
Newton unfiltered Viognier 2002

—•—

Iced Cognac Soufflé
and Wild Strawberries
Champagne Veuve Clicquot Vintage 2002

Prawn, Mango,
and Green Apple Salad

Pour all the ingredients for the dressing into a food processor
and pulse. Transfer to a bowl.

Peel the mango and cut out small balls using a scoop.
Cut the apple into thin slices and then into small sticks.

Wash the heads of lettuce, dry them, and cut in half.
Wash the chervil and dry very well.

Place the lettuce in a salad bowl, pour the dressing over,
and combine.

Arrange two pieces of lettuce in each of 6 plates.
Decorate with apple sticks and mango scoops.

Heat the oil in a pan and sauté the prawns for 5 to 6 minutes.

Arrange the hot prawns in the plates
and garnish with chervil stalks.

Serve immediately.

STARTER FOR 6

PREP 20 minutes

COOK 6 minutes

1 mango
1 Granny Smith apple
6 Romaine hearts or heads of sucrine
(Little Gem) lettuce
1 bunch chervil
3 1/2 tablespoons (50 ml) olive oil
12 raw, shelled prawns

FOR THE DRESSING
3 1/2 tablespoons (50 ml) sherry
vinegar
3 1/2 tablespoons (50 ml) water
1 tablespoon (15 ml) Dijon mustard
1/2 teaspoon (2.5 g) salt
1 pinch (1 g) pepper
2/3 cup (150 ml) olive oil
3 1/2 tablespoons (50 ml)
grapeseed oil

Sole Wafer with Morel Mushrooms and Beurre Blanc Sauce

MAIN COURSE FOR 6

PREP 35 minutes

COOK 45 minutes

¹/4 lb. (120 g) fresh salmon, filleted and skinned
1 egg white
3 ¹/2 tablespoons (50 ml) whipping cream
Fillets of 3 x 1 lb. (500 g) sole
6 large morel mushrooms
2 shallots, finely sliced
3 ¹/2 tablespoons (50 ml) olive oil
1 cup (250 ml) chicken stock
9 good-sized green asparagus
1 packet brick or phyllo pastry
Salt and pepper to taste

FOR THE BEURRE BLANC SAUCE
4 shallots, thinly sliced
1 sprig thyme
1 cup (250 ml) white wine
3 ¹/2 tablespoons (50 ml) white vinegar
¹/2 cup (125 g) butter
3 ¹/2 tablespoons (50 ml) heavy cream or crème fraîche
¹/2 bunch dill

SPECIAL EQUIPMENT
Stainless steel tubes
(1 ¹/2 inch or 4 cm diameter)

Place the salmon, egg white, and salt and pepper in the food processor. Pulse, add the whipping cream, and pulse again.

Take a piece of plastic wrap. Place a sole fillet on it, topping with 1 oz. (30 g) salmon stuffing, and cover with another sole fillet. Wrap tightly to form a tube shape. Repeat the procedure with the other sole fillets.

Wash the morel mushrooms. Soften the shallots in a saucepan with a little oil. Add the morel mushrooms and the chicken stock. Season with salt and pepper and cook for 20 minutes.

Cook the asparagus in boiling salted water for 4 to 5 minutes, depending on their thickness. Refresh them in a large bowl of iced water.

Preheat the oven to 350°F (180°C).

Cut out 6 rectangles measuring 2 ³/4 x 4 ³/4 in. (7 x 12 cm) from the brick or phyllo pastry (use double thickness if using phyllo) and brush them with oil. Roll them over 1 ¹/2 in. (4 cm) diameter metal cylinders and bake for 6 minutes.

To prepare the beurre blanc sauce, place the shallots, thyme, white wine, and white vinegar in a saucepan. Reduce the liquid by half. Dice the cold butter and incorporate the cubes, whipping all the time. Add the cream. Strain the liquid through a fine sieve and keep warm.

Steam the prepared soles for 8 minutes. Remove the plastic wrap.

Arrange the asparagus and morel mushrooms, the sole wafers, and the crisp pastry on 6 plates. Drizzle with beurre blanc sauce and garnish with sprigs of dill.

Serve immediately.

Iced Cognac Soufflé and Wild Strawberries

DESSERT FOR 6

PREP 35 minutes

COOK About 8 minutes

CHILL 4 hours

FOR THE PÂTE À BOMBE
3/4 cup (150 g) sugar
10 egg yolks

FOR THE ITALIAN MERINGUE
3 oz. or scant 1/2 cup (90 g) sugar
2 egg whites
2 sheets gelatin (see page 156)
Scant 1/2 cup (120 ml) cognac
3 cups (750 ml) whipping cream
6 small chocolate "baskets" ordered
from your pastry store (scarcely larger in
diameter than molds and 1 in. (2 cm)
higher), optional
2 punnets wild strawberries

SPECIAL EQUIPMENT
6 x tall, cylinder-shaped molds
Sugar thermometer

First prepare the pâte à bombe (the base of the soufflé). Heat the sugar with 3 1/2 tablespoons (50 ml) water in a saucepan over medium heat until it reaches a temperature of 250°F (121°C). In a large mixing bowl, beat the egg yolks using a wand blender until they turn white. Pour the cooked sugar on the egg yolks beating continuously until the mixture cools down completely.

To make the Italian meringue, heat the sugar with 2 tablespoons (30 ml) water over medium heat until the syrup reaches a temperature of 250°F (121°C). Whisk the egg whites with an electric beater until they form soft peaks. Pour the syrup over the egg whites, beating constantly until the mixture cools down completely.

Soak the sheets of gelatin in cold water for 5 minutes. Remove them from the water and drain. To dissolve the gelatin, place it in a small bowl with a tablespoon of water and microwave for 10 seconds. Pour this into the cognac, beating vigorously.

Use an electric beater to whisk the cream. Incorporate it into the Italian meringue. Carefully fold in the cognac and gelatin mixture. Then combine gently with the pâte à bombe.

Pour the preparation into tall round molds and allow to set in the refrigerator for 4 hours.

Turn the iced soufflés out of the molds and place them in the chocolate baskets, if using. Fill the baskets with wild strawberries.

If you are not using chocolate baskets, turn the soufflés on to dessert plates and garnish them with the wild strawberries.

STARTER FOR 6

PREP 30 minutes

COOK 15 minutes

CHILL 2 hours

8 bunches of mini green asparagus
8 eggs
Few drops vinegar
6 1/2 tablespoons or 3 oz. (90 g)
mayonnaise, divided
1 teaspoon (5 ml) Tabasco sauce, divided
3 sheets gelatin (see page 156)
2/3 cup (150 ml) whipping cream
3 oz. (90 g) avruga (Spanish herring roe)
Salt and pepper to taste

SPECIAL EQUIPMENT

6 small molds, 2 in. (5 cm) in diameter,
2 1/4 in. (6 cm) in height

Asparagus Charlotte and Avruga

Blanch the asparagus in a large pot of salted boiling water for 3 minutes. Refresh them in a large bowl of iced water.

Boil the eggs for 10 minutes in water to which you have added some vinegar. Cool and shell them. Separate the yolk from the white. Blend the yolks with half the mayonnaise and repeat the operation with the whites and the remaining mayonnaise. Season both with salt and pepper, adding the Tabasco.

Soak the gelatin in a bowl of cold water and drain it well. To dissolve it, place it in a small bowl with 1 tablespoon (15 ml) cream and microwave it briefly. It should not boil.

Cut the most attractive of the blanched asparagus tips to the height of the molds you are using to make the charlottes. Line the molds with the asparagus.

To make the charlotte, process the remaining asparagus together with the cut stems. Whip the cream. Fold the asparagus into the whipped cream and pour in the dissolved gelatin. Whip together and season with salt and pepper.

Place a layer of egg white mixture inside the circle of asparagus, then place a layer of egg yolk mixture within this. Fill with the asparagus mousse.

Chill for 2 hours to set.

Remove the molds, top with a spoonful of avruga, and serve.

PRECEDING DOUBLE PAGE AND RIGHT When the Baroness resided here, the salon known as the "Pontalba Salon" was decorated with lacquered panels installed by her architect, Louis Visconti. They came from the hôtel du Maine, the residence of the illegitimate son of Louis XV and his mistress, Madame de Montespan. Subsequently removed, they were eventually put back in 2001 by the government of the USA, which has played a decisive role in restoring the *hôtel particulier* to its former glory.

Roasted Rack of Pauillac Lamb, Vegetable Gratin, and Thyme-Flavored Jus

MAIN COURSE FOR 6
PREP 35 minutes
COOK 30 minutes

3 racks of lamb, frenched, or 6 chops
with French tips (ask your butcher)
(Pauillac lamb is very young,
milk-fed lamb)
Peanut oil or other neutral-flavored oil
1 cup (250 ml) lamb jus
4 sprigs thyme
Salt and pepper to taste

FOR THE VEGETABLE GRATIN
3 zucchini
10 oz. (600 g) spinach leaves
1/3 cup (70 g) butter
1 garlic clove
2 shallots, finely sliced
5 oz. (150 g) chanterelle mushrooms
7 oz. (200 g) button mushrooms
Scant 1/2 cup (100 ml)
crème fraîche or heavy cream
10 oz. (300 g) fresh chopped tomatoes

SPECIAL EQUIPMENT
6 small rectangular molds

For the vegetable gratin, trim the zucchini and slice them very finely lengthways (preferably using a mandolin). Blanch them in hot boiling water for 2 minutes and then refresh in a large bowl of iced water. Wash the spinach leaves. Sauté them rapidly in a pan with 2 $\frac{1}{2}$ tablespoons (35 g) butter. Peel the garlic clove and spear it on a fork. Dab it over the spinach to flavor it. Season with salt and pepper. Drain the spinach and chop it.

Peel and slice the shallots. Clean the mushrooms and sauté them in a skillet with 2 $\frac{1}{2}$ tablespoons (35 g) butter. Add the shallots. Pour in the cream, season with salt and pepper, and cook for 8 minutes. Blend all these ingredients in a food processor.

Line 6 small rectangular molds with the zucchini strips, overlapping them slightly. Spoon one tablespoon of chopped tomatoes into the bottom of the mold and smooth over. Place one spoonful of mushrooms and smooth over. Then spoon in a tablespoon of spinach. Fold the zucchini strips over to close the gratin.

Preheat the oven to 350°F (180°C).

Season the racks of lamb with salt and pepper. Color them on both sides in a skillet with peanut oil.

Place the racks of lamb in an ovenproof dish and cook for 9 minutes. Remove from the oven, cover with aluminum foil, and leave to rest for 4 minutes.

In the meanwhile, bake the vegetable gratins in the oven. Bring the lamb jus to the boil with the thyme and leave to infuse, covered, for 5 minutes. Remove the thyme.

Cut each rack of lamb into 2 identical pieces. Turn the vegetable gratins out of their molds.

Serve the lamb with the vegetable gratins and the sauce.

Fresh Fruit Macaroons

DESSERT FOR 6
PREP 25 minutes
BAKE 10 minutes

3/4 lb. or 4 cups (340 g)
ground almonds
9 oz. or 2 scant cups (250 g)
confectioners' sugar
8 egg whites
10 oz. or 2 generous cups (275 g)
confectioners' sugar, sifted
4 drops of red food coloring
1/2 lb. (250 g) strawberries
2 oranges
1/2 lb. (250 g) raspberries
1/2 lb. (250 g) blackberries
1 bunch lemon verbena

Preheat the oven to 350°F (180°C).
Mix the ground almonds thoroughly with the 2 scant cups (250 g)
of confectioner's sugar.

Whip the egg whites stiffly with the 2 generous cups (275 g)
of confectioners' sugar and the food coloring. Incorporate the almond-
sugar mixture into the beaten egg whites.

Spoon the batter into a pastry bag using a plain tip with a diameter
of just under 1 in. (2 cm). Line a baking sheet with parchment paper.
Pipe out 12 macaroons 2 in. (5 cm) in diameter. Bake for 10 minutes.

Remove from the oven and leave to cool on parchment paper.

Wash and hull the strawberries. If they are large, cut them in two.
Peel the oranges, ensuring there is no white pith left.
Separate into segments.

Place two macaroons on each of the 6 plates and arrange the fresh fruit
attractively around. Garnish with verbena.

STARTER FOR 6
PREP 30 minutes
COOK 20 minutes

6 slices sandwich loaf
8 Roma tomatoes
9 young carrots (with leaves)
6 mini zucchini
9 mini eggplants
1 bunch mini asparagus
1 x 1 1/2 oz. (40 g) truffle (optional)
Borage flowers, to garnish

FOR THE HERB VINAIGRETTE
1 bunch chervil
1 bunch basil
3 1/2 tablespoons (50 ml) olive oil,
preferably Kalamata
Juice of 1 lime
1 teaspoon (5 ml) balsamic vinegar
2 tablespoons (30 ml) sherry vinegar

Spring Vegetables and Herb Vinaigrette

Preheat the oven to 350°F (180°C). Cut the slices of sandwich loaf into rectangles measuring 2 x 3 in. (5 x 8 cm). Place them between two baking trays and bake for 6 minutes.

For the vinaigrette, prepare the chervil and basil leaves, reserving some for garnish. Place all the vinaigrette ingredients in the bowl of a food processor and process thoroughly until all the herbs are finely chopped.

Blanch the tomatoes in boiling water for 1 minute. Peel them and cut into quarters. Remove the cores and seeds. Cut 24 disks from the tomato flesh using a small cutter. Finely dice the remaining tomato.

Peel the carrots leaving some of the green leaves. Cut the zucchini at an angle. Cut the eggplants in two lengthways. Trim the ends of the asparagus.

Steam all these vegetables, ensuring that they remain *al dente*.

Spoon the diced tomato over the toasted bread. Drizzle with a little of the vinaigrette, and arrange the steamed vegetables and the tomato disks attractively on the toast. Spoon more vinaigrette over the vegetables. Garnish with slivers of truffle, basil leaves, and borage flowers. Serve.

PRECEDING DOUBLE PAGE On May 21, 1927, Charles Lindbergh landed at Le Bourget airport after a flight of over thirty-three hours from the USA to France. Enthusiastic Parisians gave a triumphant welcome to the first pilot to cross the Atlantic Ocean. The Lindbergh bedroom at the ambassador's residence pays tribute to the young man's extraordinary achievement, one that ushered in the development of modern transport. It is filled with souvenirs of the event: photos, US postal stamps, and a small statue of Lindbergh by the American sculptor William J. Thompson. In the hallway leading to the bedroom, a bust of the aviator is another tribute to his achievement.

Grilled Medallion of Veal, Piperade-stuffed Zucchini Blossoms, and Sage Jus

For the piperade, cut the tomatoes into quarters and de-seed them. Cut the bell peppers into quarters and remove the stems, seeds, and ribs. Slice off the ends of the zucchini and cut it into long strips. Dice the peppers, tomatoes, and zucchini. Peel and finely slice the onion and garlic cloves. Sauté the vegetables in olive oil for 5 minutes, stirring all the time. Add the thyme, cover, and cook for 10 minutes.

Remove the pistils from the zucchini flowers, ensuring that the zucchini remain attached to the blossoms, and fill them with the piperade. Steam them for 5 minutes. Slice each baby zucchini into a fan shape. Keep warm. Bring the veal jus to the boil with 3 sage leaves and boil for 3 minutes. Remove the sage leaves and keep warm.

Preheat the oven to 350°F (175°C).

Season the medallions with salt and pepper. Color them in a skillet with a little oil. Place them in an ovenproof dish and cook for 4 minutes. Allow to rest with the oven door open for 3 minutes.

Serve the veal medallions with the stuffed zucchini blossoms and the sage sauce. Garnish with small sprigs of sage.

MAIN COURSE FOR 6
PREP 30 minutes
COOK 30 minutes

6 baby green zucchini with blossoms
2 cups (25 cl) veal jus
1 bunch sage
6 x 4 oz. (120 g) veal medallions
Oil, for frying
Salt and pepper to taste

FOR THE PIPERADE
3 tomatoes
2 red bell peppers
1 yellow bell pepper
1 zucchini
1 onion
2 garlic cloves
3 1/2 tablespoons (50 ml) olive oil
2 sprigs thyme

Strawberry Pannacotta

Soak 2 gelatin sheets in a bowl of cold water.
Wash and hull $\frac{1}{2}$ lb. (250 g) of the strawberries.
Cut them into quarters and place them in a pot
with $2\frac{1}{2}$ teaspoons (10 g) sugar.
Bring to the boil and then simmer gently for 10 minutes.
Wring the water from the gelatin leaves and incorporate them into
the hot strawberry mixture. Pour into a food processor and blend.

Spoon the puree into 6 attractive glasses and chill until set
(about 2 hours).

Soak the 2 remaining gelatin sheets in a bowl of cold water
for 5 minutes. Take 2 tablespoons (30 ml) cream
and bring to the boil (you can do this in the microwave).
Drain the gelatin and dissolve it in the cream.

Whip $1\frac{2}{3}$ cup (400 ml) cream until it forms soft peaks.
Place the remaining whipping cream, the remaining sugar,
and the dissolved gelatin into a bowl. Split the vanilla beans
in two lengthways and scrape the seeds into the bowl.
Mix well. Fold the whipped cream into this mixture and beat well.
Spoon the vanilla cream into the glasses over the set
strawberry puree and chill for 2 hours.

Garnish with the remaining strawberries.

DESSERT FOR 6
PREP 20 minutes
COOK 12 minutes
CHILL 4 hours

4 sheets gelatin (see page 156)
14 oz. (400 g) strawberries
$\frac{1}{3}$ cup (60 g) sugar, divided
2 $\frac{1}{2}$ cups (200 ml) whipping cream
2 vanilla beans

FOLLOWING DOUBLE PAGE The Strawberry Pannacotta in the Louis XVI salon. The woodwork of this splendid salon are of the rare decorations that have come to us from the time of Baroness de Pontalba. The Baroness had a marked taste for classical decoration, and when her residence was being constructed, she incorporated decorative elements from *hôtels particuliers* of the rue Royale that were built in the 1780s.
PAGE 148 A detail of the tasseled curtain holders, comprising multi-bodied molds, in the Green Salon, attesting to the refinement and sophistication of the interior decoration.
PAGE 149 Champagne is often part of Chef Philippe Excoffier's menus.

Tea in the Garden

Tarte Fine with Pippin Apples,
Sparkling Lemon Cookies,
and Madeleines

SERVES 6

PREP 15 minutes

BAKE 20 minutes

4 Cox's Orange Pippin apples
1/4 lb. (250 g) ready rolled puff pastry
1 tablespoon (15 g) butter, melted
1 1/2 tablespoons (20 g)
granulated sugar

Crème fraîche or heavy cream to serve

Tarte Fine
with Pippin Apples

Preheat the oven to 350°F (180°C).
Peel and core the apples. Cut them in half,
then in quarters, and then into very thin slices.

Place the puff pastry on a baking tray.
Starting from the rim of the pastry,
arrange the apple slices in a rosette,
overlapping them slightly.
Brush the apples with the melted butter
and sprinkle with sugar. Bake for 20 minutes.

Serve warm with crème fraîche.

Sparkling Lemon Cookies and Madeleines

SERVES 6

PREP 15 minutes
CHILL 1 hour
BAKE 10 minutes

FOR THE DOUGH
3 cups (300 g) all-purpose flour
1/3 cup (60 g) sugar
1 cup (220 g) butter at
room temperature
1 pinch salt
Zest of 1 lime
Zest of 2 lemons

1 egg yolk
1/4 cup (50 g)
coarse granulated sugar

SPARKLING LEMON COOKIES

To make the dough, place all the ingredients for the dough in the bowl of a food processor and pulse for 1 minute.

Divide the dough into 2 equal parts and roll each half to form a log shape about 1 in. (2.5 cm) in diameter. Cover with plastic wrap and chill for 1 hour.

Preheat the oven to 350°F (180°C). Beat the egg yolk and brush the logs of dough using a pastry brush. Roll them in the coarse sugar.

Cut slices about 3/4 in. (1.5 cm) thick with a sharp knife. Line a baking tray with parchment paper and bake the cookies until they are a light golden color.

Allow to cool and serve with tea.

SERVES 6
(makes about 18 madeleines)
PREP 15 minutes
BAKE 8 minutes

Scant 1 1/2 cups or
9 1/2 oz (275 g) sugar
Zest of 3 lemons
5 eggs
2 1/2 cups (250 g)
all-purpose flour, sifted
2 teaspoons (8 g) baking powder
1 cup (250 g) butter, melted
and cooled

SPECIAL EQUIPMENT
Madeleine baking pan

MADELEINES

Preheat the oven to 350° F (180° C). Combine the sugar with the lemon zest.

In a mixing bowl, beat the eggs with an electric beater. Add the sugar, flour, baking powder, and cooled melted butter. Continue beating for a few minutes until the ingredients are well blended.

Butter the madeleine baking trays. Pour the batter into the molds and bake for 8 minutes. Turn the madeleines out of the molds and allow to cool.

Serve with tea.

INDEX OF RECIPES

Editor's note
Professionals prefer leaf or sheet gelatin for the smoother consistency it gives. They are generally
available in 2 gram sheets (used here) and may be bought online or at specialty stores.
The sheets must be soaked in cold water until they are completely softened. When the water is wrung out
of them, they should be gently heated until they just melt (do not boil) and then incorporated.

ACKNOWLEDGMENTS

An T. Le, Minister-Counselor for Management Affairs, U.S. Embassy, Paris
Elise Misciagna Lyons
Cathleen Lambridis Kilian
Yves Canovas
Emannuel Lacassin
Yves Roquel
César Cheicho Mendes
Antonio Pereira
Cédric Mercier
Amy Kupek Larue
The U.S. Ambassador's Residence Staff, Paris
SGT José Castro

PHOTOGRAPHIC CREDITS

All photographs in this book are by Francis Hammond with the exception of page 18:
top left © The Louisiana State Museum in New Orleans;
top right and bottom © Waddesdon Manor, The National Trust, Mike Fear.

Isabelle Clément Dreyfus and Eva Paquin would like to thank the following
boutiques who were kind enough to receive them:

Astier de Villatte
173, rue Saint-Honoré
75001 Paris

Baccarat
11, place de la Madeleine
75008 Paris

Bernardaud
11, rue Royale
75008 Paris

Christofle
9, rue Royale
75008 Paris

Cristal de Sèvres
100, avenue Charles de Gaule
92 200 Neuilly-sur-Seine

Jaune de Chrome
9-11, rue Royale
75008 Paris

J-L Coquet
9-11, rue Royale
75008 Paris

Raynaud
8 bis, rue Boissy d'Anglas
75008 Paris

and the following companies

Deshoulières www.deshoulieres.com
Dibbern www.dibbern.de
Le Jacquard français www.le-jacquard-francais.fr
Royal Limoges www.royal-limoges.fr
Wedgwood www.wedgwood.com